JOHN LESLEY
THE WORLD'S GREATEST CITIES
NEW YORK
USA
REDBACK publishing

First published 2024 by
Redback Publishing
Suite 6, 13a Narabang Way,
Belrose NSW 2085
Australia

www.redbackpublishing.com
info@redbackpublishing.com

ISBN 978-1-761400-76-6

Author: John Lesley
Editing: Caroline Thomas
Design: Redback Publishing

A catalogue record for this book is available from the National Library of Australia

Original illustrations © Redback Publishing 2024
Originated by Redback Publishing

Acknowledgements
Abbreviations: l—left, r—right, b—bottom, t—top, c—centre, m—middle. We would like to thank the following for permission to reproduce photographs: Images © shutterstock; Acknowledgements
Abbreviations: l—left, r—right, b—bottom, t—top, c—centre, m—middle. We would like to thank the following for permission to reproduce photographs: Images © shutterstock; p4bl View Apart/Shutterstock.com, p5tr Andrey Bayda/Shutterstock.com, pg6bl Just dance/Shutterstock.com, pg7tl NYC Russ/Shutterstock.com, p9tr Beyond My Ken, CC BY-SA 4.0 <https://creativecommons.org/licenses/by-sa/4.0>, via Wikimedia Commons, p9br STUDIO BONOBO TOSHIO S/Shutterstock.com, p11bl quietbits/Shutterstock.com, pg12bl cpaulfell/Shutterstock.com, pg13tr Markus Mainka/Shutterstock.com, pg14-15 MC MEDIASTUDIO/Shutterstock.com, pg15tl Stuart Monk/Shutterstock.com, pg15br Heyszilard0, CC BY-SA 4.0 <https://creativecommons.org/licenses/by-sa/4.0>, via Wikimedia Commons, pg16-17 STUDIO MELANGE/Shutterstock.com, pg17br Karolis Kavolelis/Shutterstock.com, pg19br Foolish Productions/Shutterstock.com, pg20 valerii eidlin/Shutterstock.com, pg20bl Benny Marty/Shutterstock.com, pg20br Mike Goad, Public domain, via Wikimedia Commons, pg21tr Michael Rieger, Public domain, via Wikimedia Commons, pg21br Pit Stock/Shutterstock.com, pg22t 4kclips/Shutterstock.com, pg22br Drop of Light/Shutterstock.com, pg23br Stefano Politi Markovina/Shutterstock.com, pg25t f11photo/Shutterstock.com, pg25b ItzaVU/Shutterstock.com, pg26-27 Lester Balajadia/Shutterstock.com, pg28t Debby Wong/Shutterstock.com, wp28bl Pit Stock/Shutterstock.com, pg29br Andrey Bayda/Shutterstock.com, pg30bl Oscity/Shutterstock.com, pg30tl Lewis Hine, CC0, via Wikimedia Commons, pg30mr meunierd/Shutterstock.com

CONTENTS

New York Quick Facts 4
New York's Geography 6
New York's Water Supply 8
New York's History 10
Transport in New York 12
New York's People 14
Going to School in New York 16
Wildlife in New York 18
Twin Towers 20
United Nations 22
Brooklyn Bridge 23
UNESCO World Heritage Sites in New York 24
Sesame Street 26
Broadway 28
Times Square 29
Empire State Building 30
Glossary 31
Index 32

NEW YORK QUICK FACTS

New York City is in the US state of New York. It is located on the east coast of the USA, with a large harbour that faces the Atlantic Ocean. Despite being the largest city in the USA, New York City is not the capital of its state. This honour belongs to the city of Albany.

New York City, or NYC, has more people than any other city in the USA. Its population of almost eight million people (in 2024) live in an area of 784 square kilometres. Bordering NYC is a large urban area with a population of over 20 million people.

DID YOU KNOW?

NYC is the usual abbreviation for New York City. Also known as 'The Big Apple' and 'The City That Never Sleeps', New York City is one of the world's most exciting cities.

FIVE BOROUGHS

New York City has five main sections, called boroughs. They are Brooklyn, the Bronx, Manhattan, Queens and Staten Island.

NEW YORK'S GEOGRAPHY

Three large islands make up a large part of New York City. They are Long Island, Manhattan Island and Staten Island

RIVERS

The Hudson River runs through NYC. It rises 500 kilometres away, and eventually forms an estuary when it reaches New York Harbor and the Atlantic Ocean. It was the main highway into the interior for early colonists, and has continued to be a waterway for commercial shipping. As well as the wide Hudson River, New York City also has the East River, Harlem River and Bronx River, and a number of smaller waterways.

CLIMATE

NYC experiences a very wide range of temperatures. In the winter, snow falls and there are freezing winds. In the summer, the residents sometimes swelter through heat waves.

AT THE EDGE OF A GLACIER

During the last global Ice Age, which ended about 10,000 years ago, NYC was at the edge of a giant glacier. Ice covered all of northern America, and a glacier even helped carve out the bed of the Hudson River. As the glacier began to melt, the rocks it had gathered up on its journey were dumped all across the land. Piles of these rocks now form hills across New York City.

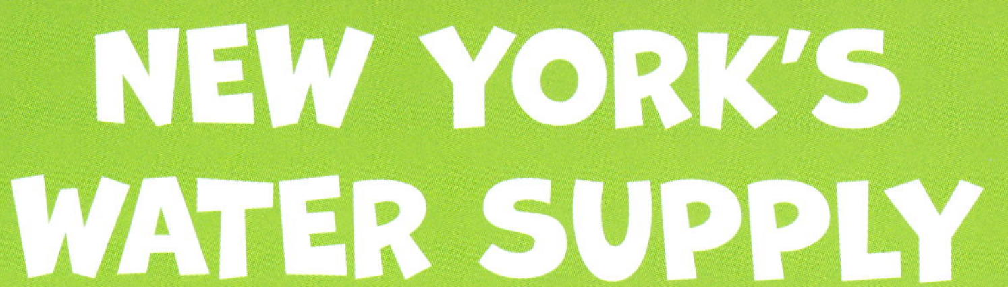

NEW YORK'S WATER SUPPLY

WATER TO DRINK

The First Nations people in the New York area used water from ponds and springs, as did the early Dutch colonists.

In the mid-1600s, the first well with a pump was provided for the general public in the city. However, as the population grew, the underground water sources became polluted, and clean water had to be found outside the city.

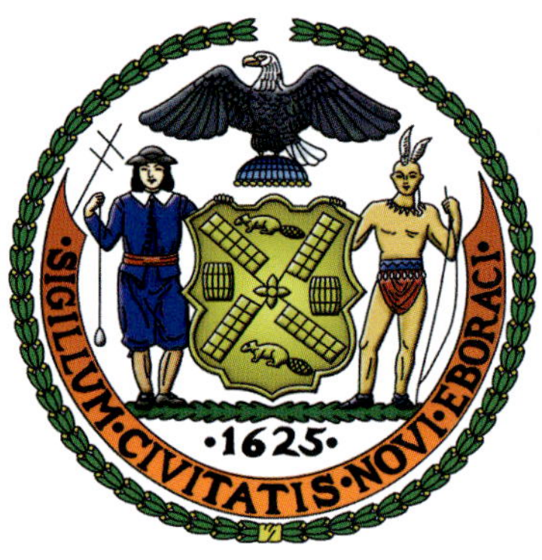

New York City official corporate insignia derived from the original city seal, first used in 1686.

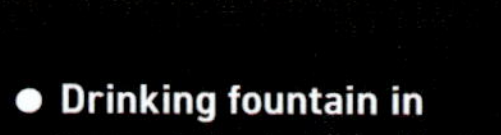

Drinking fountain in Central Park, New York

MODERN WATER TESTING

When New Yorkers turn on their taps now, the water that flows out has come from a number of reservoirs and lakes many kilometres away from the city. There are 'street-side sampling stations' throughout the city's neighbourhoods, and water is constantly tested for quality.

WATER IN THE SUMMER

New York City can be extremely hot during summer. To help its residents to cool down, people can apply to their local fire department to have the famous fire hydrants opened with a special nozzle to spray cooling mists of water. Residents can stand under the water, and children can play in it until the end of the day, when it is turned off again.

NEW YORK'S HISTORY

● New York City map published in 1664

NEW AMSTERDAM

The Lenape were the indigenous people of the New York City area.

When Dutch colonists arrived in North America in the early 1600s, they created a settlement on the island of Manhattan and called it New Amsterdam. There is a legend that the Dutch bought Manhattan Island from the Lenape people, but there is no written proof that this ever really happened.

The Dutch were after furs, in particular beaver fur, which was very popular for making hats. There were many beavers living in the waterways and forests which covered New York City before any colonists arrived.

NEW YORK

By the late 1600s, the British had taken the settlement from the Dutch, and they renamed the town New York, after the Duke of York.

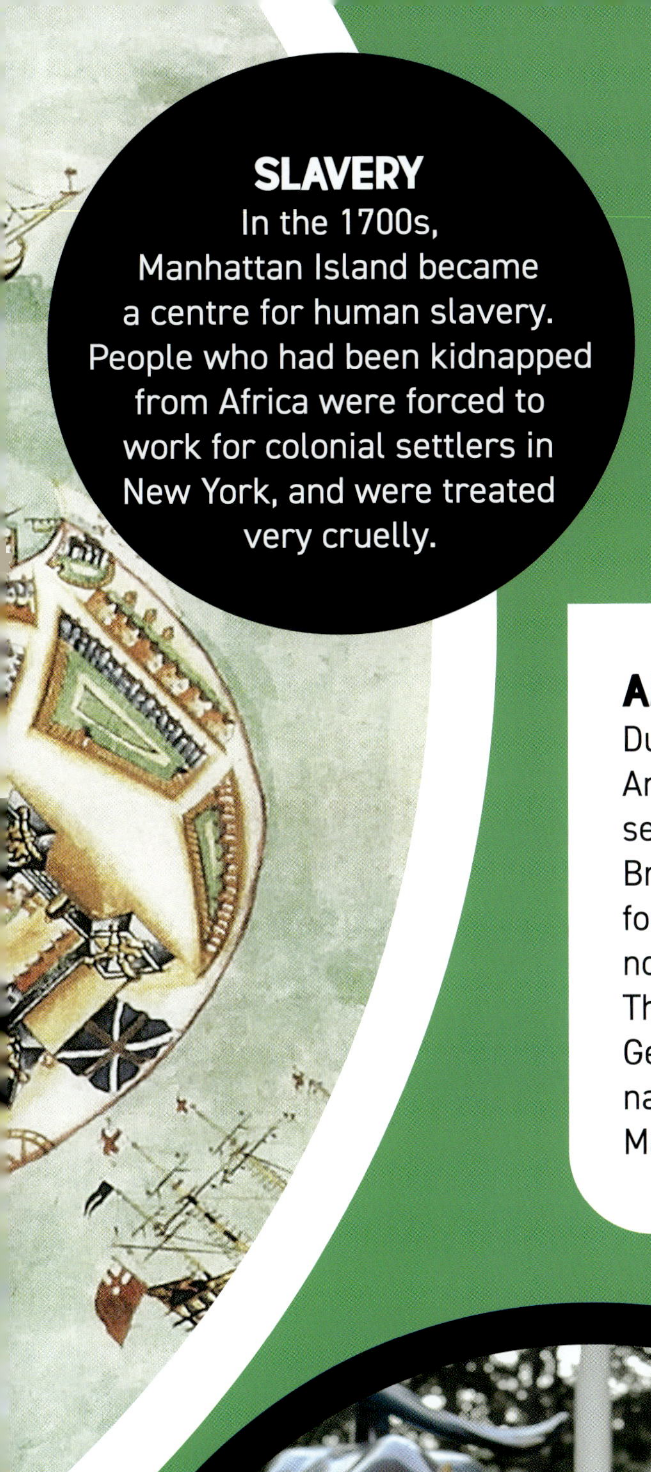

SLAVERY

In the 1700s, Manhattan Island became a centre for human slavery. People who had been kidnapped from Africa were forced to work for colonial settlers in New York, and were treated very cruelly.

George Washington statue, New York City

AMERICAN REVOLUTION

During the conflict of the American Revolution, when local settlers sought freedom from British rule, many battles were fought throughout the area which now makes up New York City. The first President of the USA, George Washington, was named at a ceremony held on Manhattan Island.

DID YOU KNOW?

Wall Street, which is one of the world's most important financial districts, was probably named after an actual wall. In the 1600s, the Dutch built a wall around their early settlement to keep out any invaders, and the street beside it became Wall Street.

TRANSPORT IN NEW YORK

SUBWAY

The New York subway was opened in 1904 and has well over 400 stations. Large sections of the system are above ground, with some parts of it built on structures that run on tracks over the tops of streets. The subway features in so many movies about New York, that even people who have never been there know a lot about it.

NEW YORK FERRIES

The people in the area of NYC have used ferries for hundreds of years. Before there were sufficient bridges to cross the many rivers that ran all through NYC, ferries were often the only reliable way to travel from one part of the city to another.

AIRPORTS

NYC needs three airports to handle the millions of passengers who come from other parts of the USA and from foreign countries every year.

The three airports that serve NYC are:

- John F. Kennedy International Airport
- LaGuardia Airport
- Newark International Airport

NEW YORK TAXIS

The yellow cabs, or taxis, are seen in almost every movie made in the city and are an iconic symbol of NYC. The yellow cabs can fill whole Manhattan streets in huge traffic jams.

NEW YORK'S PEOPLE

POPULATION

New York City has a large proportion of people who were born outside the United States. The city has been at the centre of immigration to the USA since the mid-1800s. People come from all over the world to seek refuge there, and look to New York as a place where they can find work and make their fortune.

LANGUAGES

Hundreds of languages are spoken throughout New York City, although English is the official language of the USA.

St. Patrick's Day Parade

CULTURAL INSPIRATIONS

Since the 1800s, immigrant communities have created their own distinctive neighbourhoods across New York City. The stories of Irish, Italian, Jewish and Central and South American people, as well as many others, provide great inspiration for novels, songs, movies and theatre productions.

DID YOU KNOW?

Set in NYC, *West Side Story*, a modern tale based on Shakespeare's *Romeo and Juliet*, is an acclaimed theatre production and movie. It follows the lives of people from Puerto Rico who have moved to live in NYC.

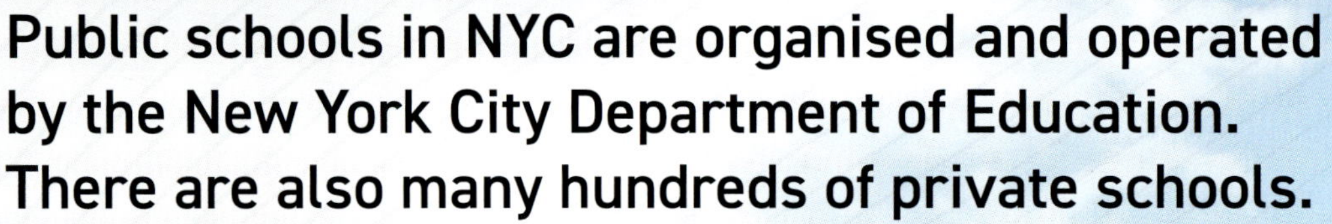

GOING TO SCHOOL IN NEW YORK

Public schools in NYC are organised and operated by the New York City Department of Education. There are also many hundreds of private schools.

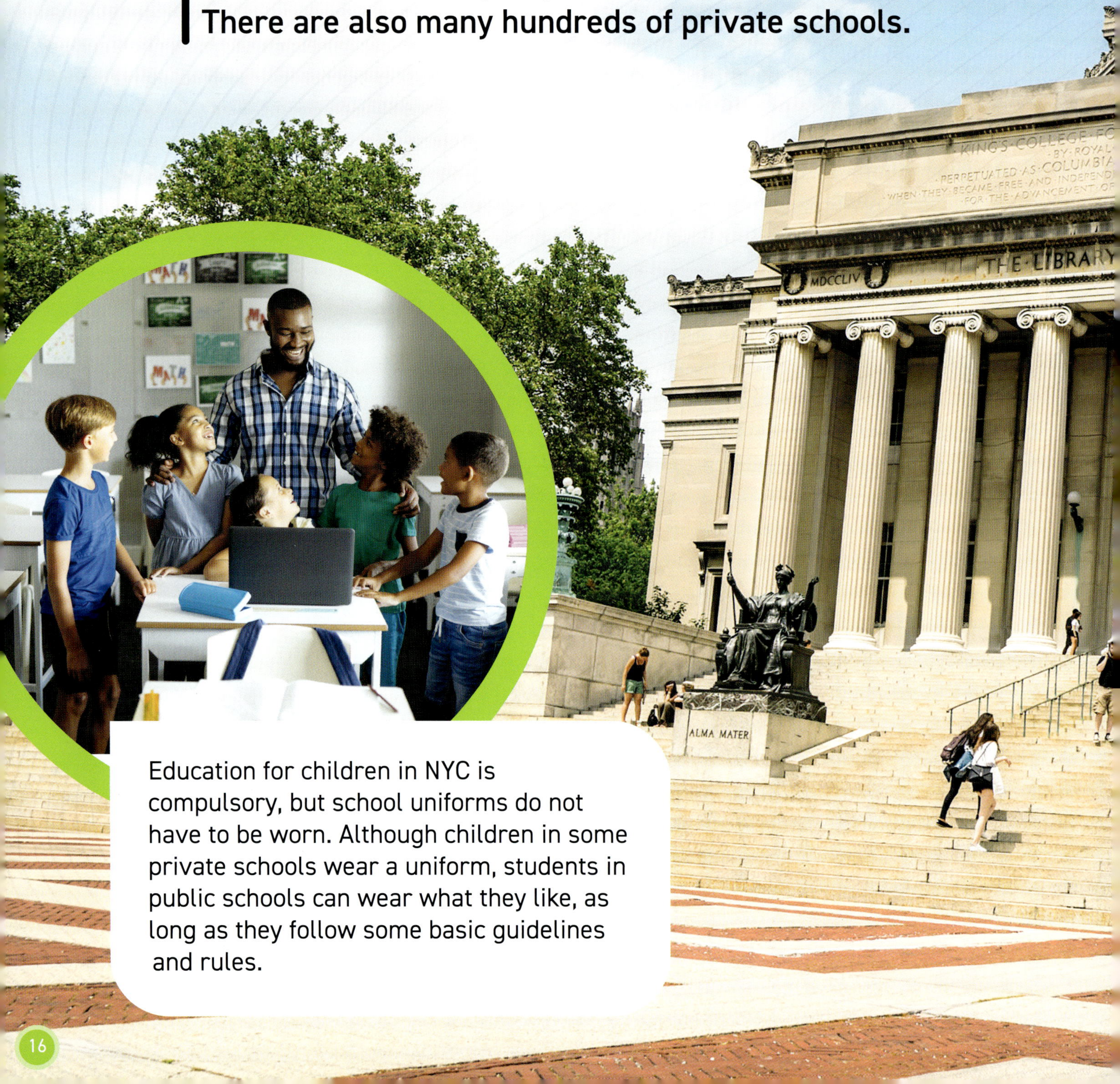

Education for children in NYC is compulsory, but school uniforms do not have to be worn. Although children in some private schools wear a uniform, students in public schools can wear what they like, as long as they follow some basic guidelines and rules.

TERTIARY EDUCATION

Universities and colleges in NYC attract students from across the USA. Both Columbia University and Cornell University are Ivy League institutions, a term which refers to their high academic standards.

Columbia University, New York

WILDLIFE IN NEW YORK

The First Nations peoples of the area now known as NYC lived in a location where there was a plentiful supply of food from the forests and rivers. Although NYC is now often referred to as a 'concrete jungle', there are still many wild animals that live in its parks and amongst its structures.

DID YOU KNOW?

The American opossum is not related to the marsupial possums that live in Australia.

CENTRAL PARK

Central Park covers a large part of Manhattan Island. It includes both natural and landscaped areas, and is a refuge for squirrels, frogs, raccoons, opossums, and chipmunks. There are many migratory birds that spend the summer in Central Park, and then fly far away to other places in the winter.

UP IN THE SKY

Bats roost under roofs, foxes build dens under buildings, and hawks fly around the canyons created by skyscrapers.

RIVERS

The huge sturgeon, a fish that can grow to over four metres in length, is a symbol of the Hudson River. Many other types of fish, as well as oysters and eels, were once abundant in the waterways, although development throughout the area has reduced their numbers.

TWIN TOWERS

On September 11, 2001, the Twin Towers were destroyed when terrorists crashed two airplanes into them, resulting in the tragic loss of thousands of innocent lives.

• "Tribute in Light", a light installation, is projected annually on the anniversary of the September 11 2001 attacks in memory of those lost

• The twin towers of the World Trade Center, circa 1980

New Yorkers were shocked by the attack on the Twin Towers, and have grieved over this disaster for decades. At the site where the Twin Towers used to stand, there is now one of the most important memorials in the United States. The National September 11 Memorial & Museum commemorates the loss of life and honours the bravery of those who helped after the attack occurred. Tourist guides showing visitors around NYC always take them to spend some time at the memorial.

The National September 11 Memorial & Museum

UNITED NATIONS

The headquarters of the United Nations (the UN) was built in 1951. It is located in NYC.

The United Nations is an organisation made up of 193 countries. They each send representatives to the UN to vote at meetings that produce important decisions regarding war, trade, human rights and assistance that should be given to struggling nations.

There are six official languages of the UN - Arabic, Chinese, English, French, Russian and Spanish. Meetings at the UN are translated into each of these languages, so that all UN members can understand what is being said. The UN needs to employ a large number of translators and interpreters.

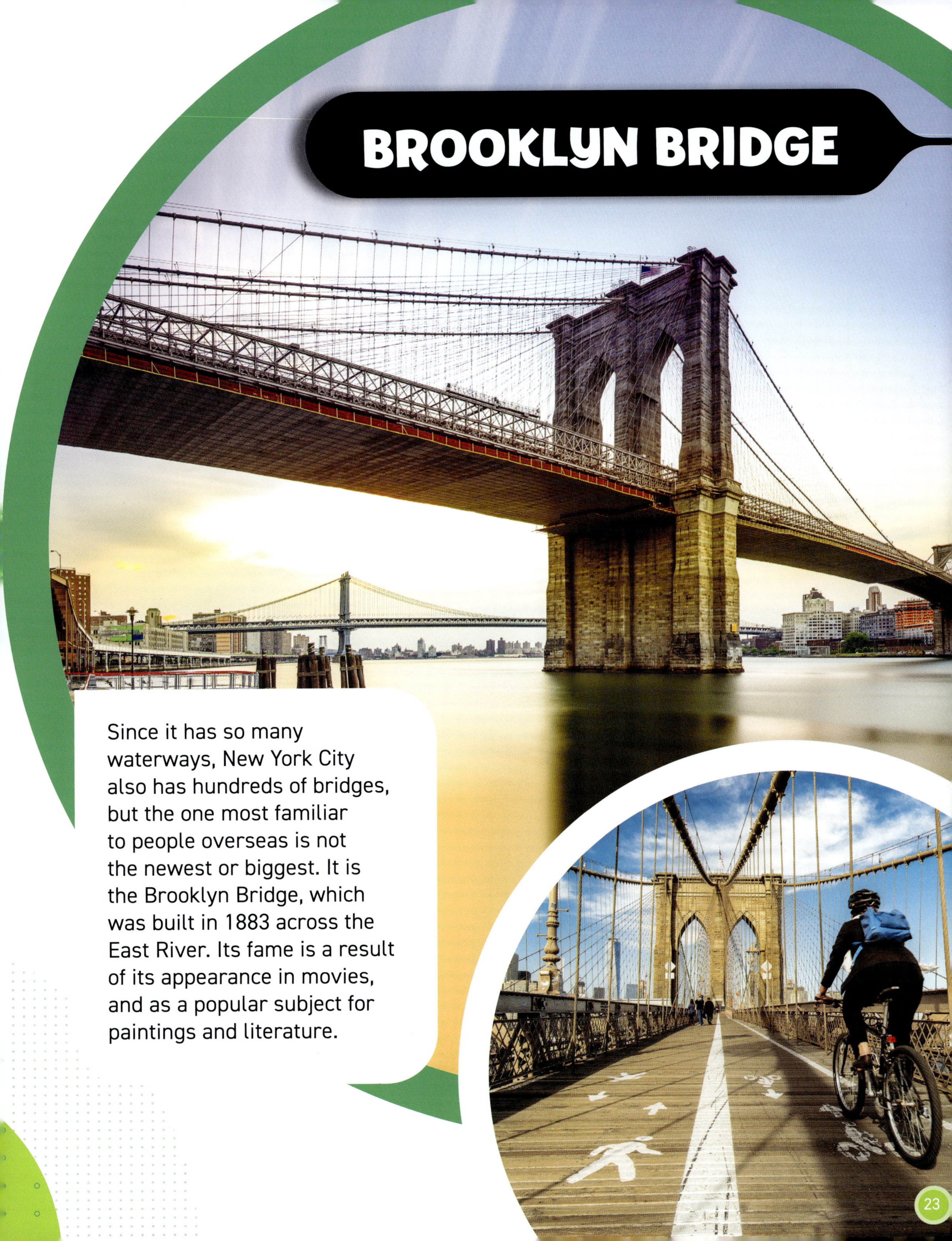

BROOKLYN BRIDGE

Since it has so many waterways, New York City also has hundreds of bridges, but the one most familiar to people overseas is not the newest or biggest. It is the Brooklyn Bridge, which was built in 1883 across the East River. Its fame is a result of its appearance in movies, and as a popular subject for paintings and literature.

UNESCO WORLD HERITAGE SITES IN NEW YORK

STATUE OF LIBERTY

The Statue of Liberty was a gift to the people of New York from the French government in the 1880s. Made from copper, and standing on Liberty Island in New York Harbor, the statue has become a symbol of freedom to New Yorkers, immigrants and people around the world. Including the pedestal, the Statue of Liberty is just over 90 metres high, and visitors can take a strenuous climb to the crown at the top.

GUGGENHEIM MUSEUM

Designed by architect Frank Lloyd Wright and completed in 1959, the Guggenheim Museum is a landmark in NYC. It has a modern art collection which attracts visitors from both NYC and overseas.

SESAME STREET

Sesame Street, the popular children's television program, has delighted children worldwide since it started in 1969. Although everyone knew it was set in New York, the makers of the show never specified a particular neighbourhood.

DID YOU KNOW?
Although Sesame Street was never a real place, New York City has now created a real place with the famous name. The intersection of West 63rd Street and Broadway is now officially known as Sesame Street.

The puppet characters sit on the front steps of apartment buildings, play in the streets, and visit small shops, all of which would be very familiar places to children living in New York City.

BROADWAY

Broadway is a long road that runs through New York. It is famous for being one of the most important places in the world for theatre and the performing arts. A successful show in one of Broadway's iconic theatres will influence the production's future success across the USA and overseas.

Beginning as a trail created by First Nations people, long before colonists arrived, Broadway is now much more than just a road. The name has come to represent the whole live theatre industry in New York City.

TIMES SQUARE

Located at the intersection of Seventh Avenue, 42nd Street and Broadway, Times Square is noted for its bright neon lighting and billboard advertising.

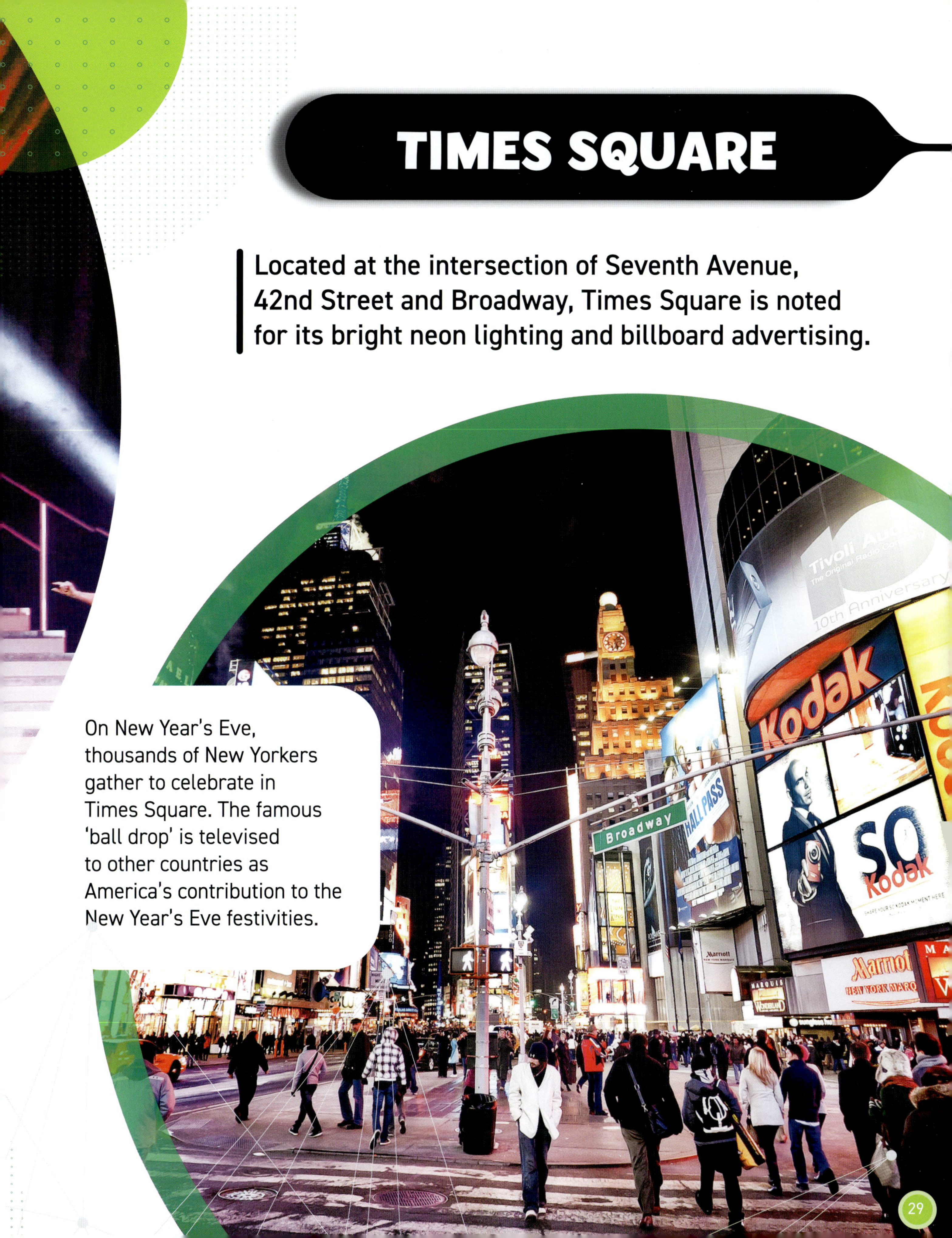

On New Year's Eve, thousands of New Yorkers gather to celebrate in Times Square. The famous 'ball drop' is televised to other countries as America's contribution to the New Year's Eve festivities.

EMPIRE STATE BUILDING

The men who built the Empire State Building did not work according to all the safety regulations that exist today.

DID YOU KNOW?
The *King Kong* movies, in which a giant gorilla escapes in New York City, use the top of the Empire State Building as a setting.

The Empire State Building was the tallest building anywhere in the world right up until the 1970s. Constructed in the early 1930s, it is now considered an architectural treasure.

GLOSSARY

billboard very large boards used for advertising beside roads and railways

canyon deep place between two high buildings

decade period of ten years

distinctive very notable for a particular quality or feature

estuary place where a river meets an ocean or sea

glacier slow-moving river of ice

iconic unique and representative of something

landscaped turned into a garden

proportion part of something

reservoir large area where water is stored

skyscraper very tall building

strenuous needing a lot of effort

urban urban referring to a city

INDEX

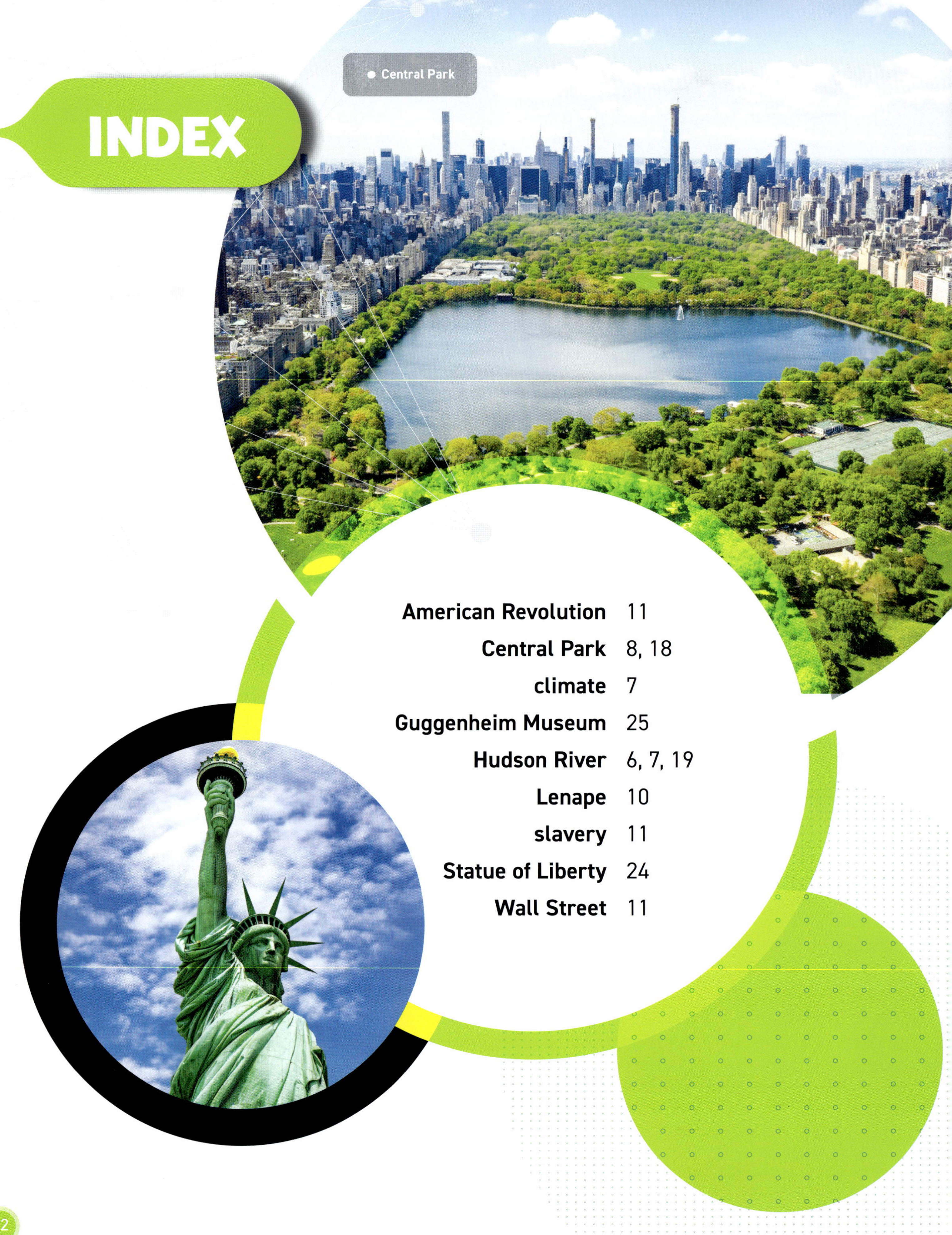

American Revolution 11
Central Park 8, 18
climate 7
Guggenheim Museum 25
Hudson River 6, 7, 19
Lenape 10
slavery 11
Statue of Liberty 24
Wall Street 11